Classic Collection

THE THREE MUSKETEERS

ALEXANDRE DUMAS

Adapted by Ronne Randall • Illustrated by Robert Dunn

QEB Publishing

D'Artagnan

It was April, 1625, and an 18-year-old boy named d'Artagnan was making his way to Paris on a knobbly old yellow horse. He wore a dusty feathered cap and carried the few coins his parents could spare. But he also had something very precious: a letter of introduction to his father's old friend Monsieur de Treville, captain of the King's musketeers. With this, d'Artagnan hoped to fulfill his one and only burning desire: to become a musketeer.

Near Orleans, outside an inn called the Jolly Miller, a gentleman with a deep scar on his face called out to d'Artagnan.

"Is that a horse or a buttercup you're riding?" he shouted, then laughed at his own joke. The men he was drinking with laughed, too.

D'Artagnan, however, was not amused. Hot-blooded and proud, he immediately leapt from his horse, drew his sword, and challenged the man to a fight.

"Foolish boy," the man said in a mocking tone. "As if I would fight a poor country boy like you." And he turned and walked away.

"Coward!" cried d'Artagnan, running after him. "You cannot insult me—or my horse—without paying for it! Come back and fight like a man!"

Suddenly a heavy blow to the back of his head sent d'Artagnan sinking to the floor. One of the innkeeper's servants, worried about a fight breaking out, had knocked him out cold.

When d'Artagnan came around, he was in a back room at the inn. His head was bandaged, and he felt bruised all over. Wincing with pain, he hobbled outside.

A short distance away, a beautiful young woman sat in a carriage. Standing beside the carriage, talking to her, was the man with the scar. D'Artagnan started toward the man, hoping he could still get his revenge. As he came closer, he overheard their conversation.

"Milady de Winter," the man was saying, "you must return to England at once."

"And what will you do?" the lady asked.

"I will return to Paris." With that, he mounted his horse and galloped away.

"False-hearted coward!" d'Artagnan cried, running after him. But it was too late. The man was gone.

D'Artagnan limped back into the inn, where he stayed overnight to recover from his injuries. The next day, when he took out his purse to pay for his food and lodging, he discovered that his letter of introduction to Monsieur de Treville was gone. He asked the innkeeper if he knew where it might be.

"I have not seen it," the innkeeper replied, "but the stranger who was here yesterday—the man with the scar—looked through your bags while you were unconscious. He must have taken it. Was it valuable?"

"Only to me," said d'Artagnan. "I will find that scoundrel and make him pay for this!"

The Mansion of Monsieur de Treville

D'Artagnan made his way to Paris, and soon found Monsieur de Treville's mansion. Inside, he saw groups of young men talking and joking with each other, and practicing their swordsmanship.

A servant told d'Artagnan to go upstairs and wait in Monsieur de Treville's chamber. Three musketeers, talking loudly together, were already there.

"Athos, you'll never believe what we heard," said one.

"What, Porthos?" asked the younger of the three.

"One of the Cardinal's spies, Rochefort, was seen disguised as a monk! Isn't that true, Aramis?" he asked the third musketeer.

"Indeed," the man replied. "And I'm sure he fooled no one. If that Rochefort crosses my path, he'll regret it."

D'Artagnan looked over at them, admiring their richly colored tunics and cloaks, and wondering who they were talking about. His thoughts were interrupted by Monsieur de Treville himself, who entered the room and motioned for the three musketeers to approach.

"I understand," Monsieur de Treville began, "that you have been dueling with the King's guards. You know that is against the law!"

"But, sir," Porthos said, "the guards attacked us."

"I did not know this," Monsieur de Treville said. "If you were defending yourselves, then you did the right thing. But see to it that you keep out of trouble."

"Yes, Monsieur," the three said together.

Monsieur de Treville then motioned for d'Artagnan to step forward. D'Artagnan told him his name and where he was from, and then explained what had happened to his letter of introduction.

"I knew your father well," Treville said. "You say that his letter to me was stolen?"

"Yes," said d'Artagnan, "by a tall man with a scar on his face."

"Hmmm…" said Treville, rubbing his chin thoughtfully. "And where did you last see this man?"

"At the Jolly Miller inn, near Orleans, Monsieur," d'Artagnan replied. "He was talking to a woman, and he told her she must return to England."

"Hmmm…" said Treville once more. "I think I know who this man is."

"Sir, just tell me where he is," said d'Artagnan eagerly. "I won't let him get away again!"

"Keep away from him," said Treville. "He is powerful and fighting him will do you no good. If you are to be a musketeer, you must learn to know your enemies."

"If I am to be…" said d'Artagnan, afraid to believe what he was hearing.

"Because I respect your father," said Treville, "I am sending you to the Royal Academy for training. You can become a musketeer, but you must prove yourself first."

"I shall, Monsieur," said d'Artagnan gratefully. "You will not regret your decision."

Athos, Porthos, and Aramis

When Monsieur de Treville sat down to write a letter introducing d'Artagnan to the director of the Academy, d'Artagnan glanced out of the window. On the street below, a familiar-looking man was walking by.

"There he is!" he cried.

"Who?" asked Monsieur de Treville, looking up.

"The man from the Jolly Miller!" spluttered d'Artagnan. "He won't escape from me this time!" And he rushed out of the room, leaving Monsieur de Treville shaking his head in disapproval.

As he sprinted down the stairs, d'Artagnan bumped into a musketeer, slamming him against the wall. The musketeer shouted in surprise and pain.

"Excuse me, excuse me," d'Artagnan muttered, pushing past him. But he did not get very far. The musketeer seized his arm.

"You are in a great hurry!" he said angrily.

D'Artagnan saw that it was the musketeer called Athos. "I'm terribly sorry, sir," he said. "I did not mean to hurt you or act rudely. But I really am in a great hurry. I have to find someone."

"Whether you meant to or not, you have behaved extremely rudely!" Athos scolded him. "And you won't have to bump into anyone else to find me. I challenge you to a duel, tomorrow at noon, at the old convent."

"I accept your challenge," said d'Artagnan. "And I will be there at ten to twelve!" Then he rushed off.

D'Artagnan raced out into the street, but ran into Porthos, who was talking to a soldier.

"What is wrong with you?" cried Porthos.

"Excuse me," said d'Artagnan. "I was in a great hurry."

"You cannot treat a musketeer this way," said Porthos. "I challenge you to a duel—one o'clock tomorrow, at the old convent!"

Agreeing hastily, d'Artagnan rushed off, but he had lost the thief. As he walked back, he began feeling ashamed. He had acted like a fool in front of Monsieur de Treville and two musketeers whom he admired.

Suddenly, he saw an opportunity to make things better. Right in front of him was Aramis, talking to three guards. He had just dropped his handkerchief, and d'Artagnan rushed over to pick it up.

"I believe this is yours," said d'Artagnan with a bow. Aramis grabbed it angrily, and only then did d'Artagnan see it was a lady's handkerchief.

"Ah," laughed one of the guards. "I see that Madame de Bois has lent you her handkerchief, Aramis. Do you still insist that there is nothing between you?"

Aramis, his face red with anger, turned to d'Artagnan. "How dare you interfere in my personal affairs?" he growled at him. "I challenge you to a duel—two o'clock tomorrow, at the old convent!"

The Musketeers and the Cardinal's Guards

The next day, as he hurried to the old convent, d'Artagnan hoped he didn't look as nervous as he felt. He was about to fight not one, but three of the most skilled swordsmen in Paris, if not in all of France.

D'Artagnan wondered whether he should beg for forgiveness, but he knew there was no honor in begging.

Athos was waiting for him. "Are you alone?" he asked. "Have you not brought a second with you?" A second was someone who would stand up for a gentleman in a duel, and make sure the fight was fair.

"I know no one in Paris," said d'Artagnan, "but I can stand up for myself."

"I regret having to kill a friendless man," said Athos. "I myself have asked two friends to act as my seconds, but they seem to be late."

Then Porthos and Aramis came striding toward them. "You're late!" said Athos.

"You're early!" cried d'Artagnan, in the same instant.

"What?" said everyone together.

The situation was soon explained, and d'Artagnan and Athos faced each other for the first duel.

But their swords had barely touched when a pack of the Cardinal's guards swooped down on them.

"Put down your swords!" cried their leader, a man named Jussac. "You know full well that dueling in public is illegal. I therefore am placing all four of you under arrest—unless you wish to fight us, of course!"

The three musketeers knew that Monsieur de Treville would never forgive them if they were arrested.

"There are five of them and only three of us," Athos whispered, "but we have no choice—we must fight."

"Excuse me," d'Artagnan said. "There are four of us."

"You are not a musketeer," Porthos said.

"Perhaps not," d'Artagnan replied, "but I have the heart and soul of a musketeer. I will not desert you!"

"Then forward, men!" cried Athos.

The courtyard echoed with the sound of steel on steel as sword blades clashed. D'Artagnan, thrilled that he was actually fighting beside the King's musketeers, moved with the speed and fury of a tiger. The guards did not know which way to turn. Aramis's sword went straight through one of his opponents. Athos and Porthos were both hit—Porthos in the arm, Athos in the shoulder—but this made them fight even more fiercely.

Finally Jussac called a halt. He had been injured by d'Artagnan and had already lost one man; he did not want to lose any more. Defeated, he and the remaining guards left the courtyard.

The three musketeers gathered around their new friend and asked his name.

"D'Artagnan," he told them, "and if I am not a musketeer yet, I am the next best thing—your loyal friend and companion. All for one and one for all!"

"All for one and one for all!" the three musketeers replied, and the four men raised their swords in a salute.

His Majesty King Louis XIII

Monsieur de Treville felt he had to scold the musketeers for fighting after he had warned them not to. In private, however, he congratulated them and told them he was proud of their courage. He knew the Cardinal's guards had goaded them into fighting. He was especially proud of young d'Artagnan for his loyalty to his newfound comrades.

He also made sure the King, Louis XIII, knew exactly what had happened. The King was so impressed that he asked Treville to bring all four men to the palace to meet him. When they were presented to him, the King was shocked to see that d'Artagnan was so young.

"Monsieur de Treville," he said, "you told me he was a young man—but he is no more than a boy! And are you the one who wounded Jussac so badly?" he asked d'Artagnan.

"Yes, Your Majesty," d'Artagnan replied proudly.

"Such valor requires a reward," the King said. "You are not yet ready to be a musketeer, but I hope you will work hard at your training. Your trustworthiness will be a great credit to the Academy."

He also gave d'Artagnan a prize of forty gold coins. As soon as they left the palace, d'Artagnan shared out the money with Athos, Porthos, and Aramis.

"After all," he said, "I am not the only one who fought valiantly that day."

The three musketeers and d'Artagnan were soon the best of friends. The musketeers taught d'Artagnan about life in Paris, and explained the workings of the court of King Louis and his wife, Queen Anne. D'Artagnan was now more eager than ever to be a musketeer himself.

One afternoon, d'Artagnan's landlord, Monsieur Bonacieux, knocked on his door. He was distressed, and told d'Artagnan that his wife, Constance, had been kidnapped. Some neighbors had seen her being bundled into a carriage by a tall man with a scar on his face.

Hearing the word 'scar,' d'Artagnan began to listen more closely. This was certainly the man he had been looking for since he arrived in Paris!

"I am so worried," Bonacieux fretted. "Constance is Queen Anne's seamstress, and she knows many secrets about her. Perhaps you and your musketeer friends can help me rescue my wife?"

From what the musketeers had told him, d'Artagnan knew that some of the Queen's secrets must be about her marriage to the King, which had never been happy. She loved the Duke of Buckingham, and he was in love with her. D'Artagnan also knew that the Cardinal was the Queen's enemy, and would do anything to get her into trouble with the King. The man with the scar was one of the Cardinal's accomplices.

"I will do everything I can to find your wife," d'Artagnan promised his landlord. "My musketeer friends will be here soon. You can count on their help as well."

The Duke of Buckingham

By the time the musketeers arrived, Bonacieux himself had been arrested by the Cardinal's guards. D'Artagnan told his friends what had happened.

They decided that d'Artagnan would keep watch at the house and Athos would visit Monsieur de Treville, to find out if he knew anything. Porthos and Aramis went their separate ways to see what they might discover.

D'Artagnan carefully watched everything that happened in the street below his window. By late evening, he had seen nothing, and he was about to go to bed when he heard someone knocking on the door downstairs, and then a scuffle in the apartment below.

Grabbing his sword, d'Artagnan rushed downstairs and broke into the apartment. The scar-faced man and three others were trying to tie up a beautiful and very frightened young woman. Seeing d'Artagnan with his sword raised, they fled.

The woman was Constance Bonacieux. She had escaped from her kidnappers and had sneaked home, unaware that she had been followed.

Constance thanked d'Artagnan for rescuing her. D'Artagnan told her that her husband had been arrested.

The news upset her greatly. "I thought he might be able to protect me," she said. "I have a dangerous errand to do, and I must do it tonight. Will you help me?"

Looking into Constance Bonacieux's deep-blue eyes, d'Artagnan knew he would do anything she asked.

Constance rushed through the dark streets, with d'Artagnan close behind her. Near the river, at the foot of a bridge, a man came out of the shadows to greet her.

"This is the Duke of Buckingham," she explained. "He has traveled from England to see Queen Anne."

"If you would follow us," the Duke said, "and make sure that no one attacks us, we would be most grateful."

D'Artagnan followed them all the way to the palace, where Constance led them through a series of secret passages to the Queen's private rooms.

When the Queen arrived, her eyes sparkled like emeralds. But her face was drawn and pale with worry.

"It is too risky for you to be here," she told the Duke.

"I would risk anything to see you," he told her. "You know how much I love you."

"Please go back to England," she begged him, "until we can find some way for you to come here that does not put your life in danger."

"I will," he promised, "but only if you give me something of yours by which I can remember this meeting, so I know it wasn't a dream."

The Queen whispered something to one of her servants, who fetched a small rosewood box.

"Here," said the Queen. "Take this, and go!"

The Duke kissed the Queen's hand and then left, clutching the box. He met Constance and d'Artagnan in the passageway outside, and the three left the palace.

Men of the Robe and Men of the Sword

Nobody knew that one of the Queen's maids was actually a spy for the Cardinal. She immediately told the Cardinal everything she had seen and heard. She also told him what was inside the rosewood box: twelve diamond studs that the King had given to Queen Anne.

The Cardinal immediately came up with a plan to trap the Queen and reveal her secret to the King.

First he wrote a letter to Milady de Winter in London, telling her to attend the next ball where she might see the Duke of Buckingham. He told her to look for the diamond studs on the Duke's tunic, and to cut off two and send them to him. He then persuaded King Louis to give a ball in the Queen's honor.

"What an excellent idea!" said the King. "She can wear the diamond studs I recently gave her." This was just what the Cardinal hoped he would say.

When the King told his wife about the ball, and asked her to wear the diamonds, she grew very anxious.

"What shall I do?" she tearfully asked Constance.

"Write to the Duke and ask him to return the diamonds," Constance said. "My friend d'Artagnan can be trusted to take the letter to London and deliver it."

D'Artagnan, of course, was only too happy to help the lovely Constance. She was deeply grateful, and assured him that the Queen would reward him handsomely.

"Knowing that I am helping you and my Queen is all the reward I need," he told her.

D'Artagnan went straight to Monsieur de Treville to explain.

"I must go to London for a short while," he said. "I have secret business to conduct for the Queen. Her honor—perhaps even her life—may be at stake."

Monsieur de Treville's expression grew serious.

"I will not ask you to reveal the secret," he said. "Guard it with your life. But a mission of this sort is dangerous, so I cannot let you go alone. Athos, Porthos, and Aramis will accompany you."

D'Artagnan would have carried out the mission on his own, but he was relieved and pleased that his friends would be coming with him.

"A thousand thanks for your goodness, sir," he said, as Monsieur de Treville began to write messages for d'Artagnan to take to the musketeers.

Although d'Artagnan thought his mission was secret, there was someone else who knew about it. Constance's husband, Monsieur Bonacieux, had been released from prison on condition that he act as a spy for the Cardinal.

Of course he told no one of this arrangement, not even his wife. Thinking she could trust him, Constance told him that their tenant d'Artagnan would be taking a letter to London for the Queen.

Bonacieux immediately told the Cardinal—and plans to stop d'Artagnan were soon under way.

The Journey

D'Artagnan and the musketeers left Paris in the middle of the night, under cover of darkness. The roads leading out of the city seemed empty and quiet, but the four men knew how dangerous their journey was, and they feared an ambush by the Cardinal's spies at every turn. As the sun rose, however, their spirits brightened.

By eight o'clock in the morning, they had reached the town of Chantilly, where they decided to stop for breakfast and to give their horses a rest.

They found a small tavern, where a servant took their horses away to give them food and water.

"Don't take off their saddles," said Porthos. "We need to be ready to leave quickly."

There was another man in the tavern's dining room, and they had a polite conversation with him about the weather and the state of the roads. Then, just when they were getting up to go, the man grabbed Porthos and proposed a toast to the Cardinal's health.

"I will gladly drink the Cardinal's health," said Porthos, "if you will also toast the King's health."

The man refused, then drew his sword and challenged Porthos to a duel.

"Don't do anything foolish," Athos whispered. "Just deal with him quickly and let's go."

"This will take as long as it has to," Porthos replied, drawing his own sword. "Go on without me—I'll catch up with you!"

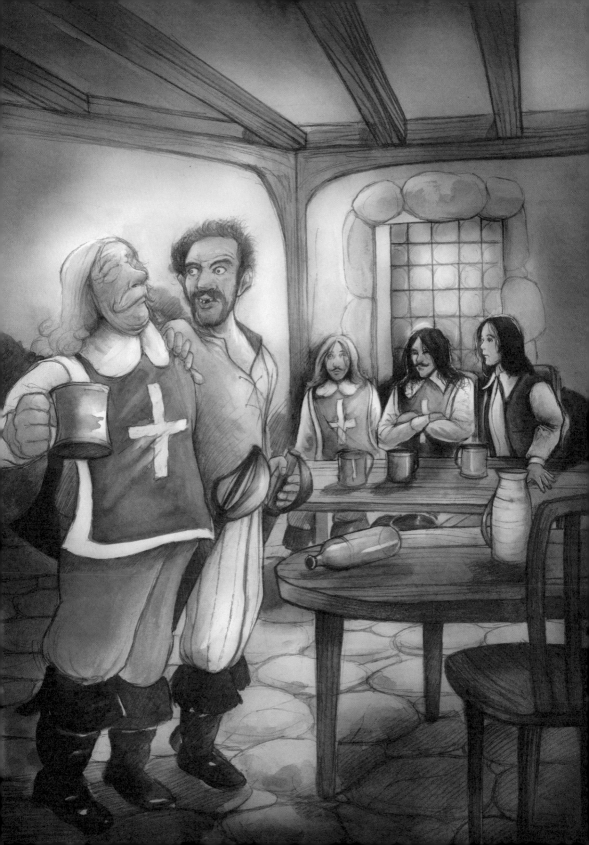

D'Artagnan, Aramis, and Athos rode off, certain that Porthos would win the fight quickly and catch up with them before long. But by the time they were approaching the town of Beauvais, there was still no sign of him.

"Let's wait for a while," Athos suggested. "Surely Porthos can't be too far behind us now."

They stopped and waited for two hours, but Porthos did not appear, and there was no word from him. So they went on with their journey.

Just outside the town, some men were digging at the side of the road, which made it difficult for them to get by. Aramis grew so impatient and angry that he began shouting at the workers. Athos tried to restrain him, but it was too late—the men began throwing stones at them. While they were dodging the stones, one of the workmen reached into a trench and pulled out a musket.

"It's an ambush!" cried d'Artagnan. "Let's get out of here!"

Spurring their horses on, the three galloped away. But Aramis had been shot, and his shoulder was badly wounded. As they rode on, he grew paler and weaker.

After two hours, Aramis said he could not go any farther, and he begged the others to leave him at the next inn they came to. "I'll be all right," he told them. "I'll wait here for Porthos."

D'Artagnan and Athos had no choice. After making sure Aramis was safe, they mounted their horses and rode away.

The Duke and the Diamonds

Athos and d'Artagnan rode on toward the coast. They changed their route several times to confuse anyone who might be following them. They were certain their misfortunes had not happened by chance—the Cardinal had sent his men after them.

Late that night, they reached the town of Amiens, where they found an inn to stop at overnight.

The innkeeper came to the door and grumpily showed them to a room. Once inside, Athos and d'Artagnan barricaded the door, and took turns sleeping so that one of them could keep watch at all times.

In the morning, d'Artagnan and Athos went to pay for their lodgings. They found the landlord sitting at a desk in a back room.

"Here is what we owe," said Athos, giving him several coins. The landlord turned the coins over in his hand. "These are counterfeit," he said. "If you don't give me genuine coins, I'll have you both arrested."

"You rascal!" exclaimed Athos. "You know as well as I do those coins are real."

Suddenly the innkeeper pulled a pistol out of a drawer and shouted for help. Three armed men rushed in and grabbed Athos.

"I'm trapped!" Athos shouted. "Run, d'Artagnan!" D'Artagnan fled for his life. He grabbed his horse and galloped toward the port of Calais, where he would get the ferry to England.

In Calais, d'Artagnan quickly made for the harbor, where he was told that, by order of the Cardinal, no one could board the ferry without a letter of permission from the governor of the port. D'Artagnan did not have enough time to apply for a letter—the ferry was due to leave in less than half an hour. Desperate, he pleaded with another traveler for his letter. When the man refused, d'Artagnan drew his sword and challenged him to a fight. It was a difficult battle, but d'Artagnan won and, with his newly acquired letter, quickly boarded the ferry.

Worn out, d'Artagnan slept for nearly the entire journey across the Channel, and woke the next morning to see the cliffs of Dover coming into view. He reached London late that afternoon. Though he knew almost no English, he could say "Duke of Buckingham," and was soon shown the way to the Duke's home.

When the Duke read the letter d'Artagnan had brought, he immediately got the rosewood box. But when he opened it, his eyes grew wide with shock. Two of the diamond studs were missing!

At first the Duke was baffled. Who could have stolen them, and how? Then he remembered that the one time he had worn the studs—to a ball at Windsor, a week earlier—Milady de Winter had been there, and had been especially friendly with him.

"She distracted me, and then somehow took the diamonds," he said angrily. "That woman is treacherous —and I am sure she is working for the Cardinal!"

The Return

Both the Duke and d'Artagnan knew if the Queen was not wearing all twelve diamonds at the ball, the King would be furious. The ball was in five days. The Duke sent for the best jeweler in London, who said he needed only two days to make two exact copies.

D'Artagnan stayed at the Duke's home for the next two days, as a privileged guest. The jeweler stayed there as well—the Duke set up a workshop for him, so that he would not be distracted by any other duties.

At eleven o'clock on the second day, the new diamond studs were ready—and they were perfect. But that very morning, an order was issued forbidding any English ships from leaving for France, as the two countries were on the brink of war. The Duke promised he would get d'Artagnan home safely. He arranged for a small private boat to take d'Artagnan to the small town of St. Valery in France. There, d'Artagnan was to go to a wine store and say a secret password. On hearing it, the owner would provide d'Artagnan with a horse and directions to Paris. D'Artagnan was to make four stops along the way and, when he repeated the password, he would be given whatever he needed to continue the journey safely.

"Nothing will be allowed to get in the way of your delivering these diamonds to Queen Anne," the Duke assured him. "You have my word."

By the time d'Artagnan got to Paris, the ball was just hours away. The city was buzzing with excitement. At the palace, preparations had been going on for days, and crowds had gathered outside, hoping to catch a glimpse of the guests as they arrived.

There were crowds inside the palace as well—all waiting eagerly for the King and Queen to emerge from their dressing chambers and enter the ballroom.

The Cardinal approached the King just outside the ballroom, and showed him the two diamonds Milady de Winter had sent him. "Watch your wife carefully," he said, "and count the diamonds. She will be missing two. Ask her where they have gone—she will be forced to confess that she has been deceiving you."

"Deceiving me?" roared the King. "How dare you suggest such a thing!"

"Wait and see," said the Cardinal.

The King entered the ballroom, and the Queen soon followed. All the guests gasped in admiration at her beautiful gown. But the King was shocked to see that she was not wearing her diamonds at all. When he questioned her, she said, "Sire, with the great crowds, I feared they might be damaged or lost. But I will fetch them if you wish."

She left at once, with Constance close beside her. She was in a great rush, and did not notice the sly, knowing smile on the Cardinal's face—or the two diamond studs he was holding.

The Four Musketeers

A few moments later, the Queen and Constance returned to the ballroom. A ribbon of glittering diamonds now sparkled around the Queen's neck. She stood calmly before the King and the Cardinal.

"I see you are wearing all twelve studs," said the King.

"Of course," the Queen replied. Then, seeing the two the Cardinal was holding, added, "Do you mean to give me two more? Fourteen diamonds is a very generous gift!"

His face reddening, the King turned to the Cardinal and said angrily, "What is the meaning of all this?"

The Cardinal, looking sheepish, said, "Forgive me. I only meant to offer these two diamonds to Her Majesty as a gift."

The Queen smiled at the Cardinal, and graciously accepted the diamonds.

"Thank you so much, Your Eminence," she said. "I am all the more grateful, as I am sure these two diamonds cost you more than the other twelve cost His Majesty." The look on her face told the Cardinal that she knew all about his wicked plot. Then, with a curtsy to both the King and the Cardinal, the Queen and Constance turned and left.

Standing quietly in a corner of the ballroom, watching everything, was d'Artagnan, who had delivered the two new diamonds to the Queen just in the nick of time.

A few moments later, Constance returned to the ballroom to fetch d'Artagnan. She led him down a long passageway to a private room, where the Queen and another servant were waiting. The Queen looked radiant and happy, and smiled as d'Artagnan entered.

Seeing the Queen, d'Artagnan immediately bowed his head and dropped to one knee before her. Queen Anne took d'Artagnan's hand and, without anyone else seeing, put something into it. Then, quickly and quietly, she left the room.

Holding his breath, d'Artagnan looked at what the Queen had given him: it was a small box containing a splendid ring and a note of thanks from the Queen herself. D'Artagnan was thrilled.

The next morning, he was summoned by Monsieur de Treville.

"Congratulations are in order," said Treville. "I saw the King and Queen at the ball last night, and from the joy on their faces—and the sour expression worn by the Cardinal—I must assume that you carried out your mission with admirable success."

"It was an honor to serve my Queen, sir," d'Artagnan replied. He then told him of the adventures he and the three musketeers had met with on their way to London.

"I have heard from the others," Treville said. "They are all safe and well, and all three are on their way back to Paris."

"Then my happiness is complete," d'Artagnan replied.

When d'Artagnan returned home, Constance Bonacieux was waiting for him. "I cannot thank you enough for all you have done," she said.

"I would stop at nothing to help my Queen," d'Artagnan replied, "or you. Though we can never be more than friends, I will love you always."

"Thank you," she said, taking his hand. From the tears in her eyes, d'Artagnan could see his feelings were returned. Constance was married to someone else—but knowing she loved him was enough.

A few days later, at Monsieur de Treville's mansion, d'Artagnan was reunited with the musketeers. They were happy to see each other and all had exciting stories to tell. D'Artagnan's heart was overflowing. He had served his Queen, gained the friendship of these admirable men, and won the heart—if not the hand—of the woman he loved. He could not have asked for more.

But Monsieur de Treville did have one more piece of news for him. "In recognition of your service to your Queen," he said, "and of your gallantry, bravery, and loyalty to your comrades, I am pleased to welcome you into the company of the King's musketeers."

For a moment, d'Artagnan just stared at him. Then he stammered, "Y-you mean…"

"Yes!" Athos burst out. "You are one of us now!"

And as his fellow musketeers gathered around him, all four put up their swords and chorused, "All for one and one for all!"

About the Author

Alexandre Dumas was born on July 24, 1802 in Picardy, France. After his father died, his mother could not provide a good education for the young Alexandre, but he was still passionate about reading. Alexandre's vivid imagination for adventure was inspired by tales of his father's bravery in Napoleon's army. In later life, Alexandre wrote articles for magazines, plays for the theater, and eventually novels, at which he was very successful. He continued to write until his death in 1870.

Other titles in the Classic Collection series:

Editor: Lauren Taylor
Designer: Izzy Langridge
Cover typography: Matthew Kelly

Copyright © QEB Publishing, Inc. 2011

First published in the United States in 2011 by
QEB Publishing, Inc.
3 Wrigley, Suite A
Irvine, CA 92618

www.qed-publishing.co.uk

Library of Congress Cataloging-in-Publication Data

Randall, Ronne.
 The three musketeers / by Alexandre Dumas ; retold by Ronne Randall.
    p. cm. -- (Classics collection)
 Summary: A shortened, simplified version of an adventure in seventeenth-century France, when young d'Artagnan initially quarrels with, then befriends, three musketeers and joins them in trying to outwit the enemies of the king and queen.
 ISBN 978-1-60992-034-0 (library bound)
1. France--History--Louis XIII, 1610-1643--Juvenile fiction. [1. France--History--Louis XIII, 1610-1643--Fiction. 2. Adventure and adventurers--Fiction.] I. Dumas, Alexandre, 1802-1870. The three musketeers. II. Title.
 PZ7.R1584Tj 2012
 [E]--dc22
                                    2010053354

ISBN 978 1 60992 296 2 (hardback)

Printed in China